AF327435

Trunks of the Gunks

Trunks of the Gunks

Photographs by Nora Scarlett

A visual odyssey through the Shawangunk Mountains.

An endeavor to see beyond the ordinary into a forest of surprise and delight.

A testimony to how life persists despite adversity and how it succeeds in astonishing ways.

BLACK · DOME

Published by Black Dome Press Corp.
649 Delaware Ave., Delmar, N.Y. 12054
blackdomepress.com
(518) 439-6512

Copyright © 2016 Nora Scarlett
norascarlett.com

Without limiting the rights under copyright above, no part of this publication may be
reproduced, stored in or introduced into a retrieval system, or transmitted, in any form,
by any means (electronic, mechanical, photocopying, recording, or otherwise), without the
prior written permission of the publisher of this book.

ISBN 13: 978-1883789862
Library of Congress Control Number: 2016956744

Design: Toelke Associates, Chatham, NY
toelkeassociates.com

Map artwork by Amelia Toelke

Author photograph by Zoe Borris

Dedicated to my father
ROBERT MICHAEL SCARLETT

Wisdom begins in wonder

Socrates

Every now and then someone comes along who looks at things in a different way, with a diferent eye so to speak. Nora Scarlett is one of those people.

Most of us who frequent the Shawangunks know it as a special place. For some 200 years people have been attracted to its craggy, picturesque grandeur, its history, and — more recently — its opportunities for physically challenging activities. A few of us as naturalists have had the privilege of observing its ecosystem up close. We all have our favorite locations and subjects. Many of us have a special affinity for trees.

In 1990 Keith Smiley of Mohonk, in his booklet *The Importance of Trees*, expressed his feeling for trees this way: "It is a special joy to roam the woods on the Shawangunk ridges and find many kinds of trees. ... Unlike birds and wild animals, trees stand still and invite repeated visits. Not only do they become old friends, but they also provide ample opportunity to exercise the human senses of touch and taste and smell and hearing. Overworked eyes used as a means of relating and identifying can be given a rest in making friends with trees."

As Keith implies, we are privileged to roam the Shawangunk ridges that today are mostly covered by forest. That wasn't the case not many decades ago, however, when much of the forest was cut to supply the demand for wood products and byproducts, a gradual deforesting that began with the first settlement on the ridge starting about 1800. These environmentally devastating industries of the nineteenth and early twentieth centuries included harvesting tanbark, hoop poles, lumber, charcoal, and cordwood, as well as clearing the land for agriculture. Major forest fires consumed the residue. Documentary photographs and written accounts are startling in what they reveal about the scope and the intensity of the forest cutting.

By the 1920s and 1930s the local demand for wood had evaporated, replaced by other, cheaper fuels, chemical products, and steel. At the same time there was a diminishing need for large, land-intensive farms, including dairy. The forest regenerated on the slopes and ridges of the Shawangunks, and much of the land returned to a state of wildness. Many of the trees that we see today grew from that period. Some of our oldest trees, dating to the early seventeenth century, survived the industrial onslaught only because they were in a difficult location to access or because of their small economic return.

I often think of the difficulty of being a tree, as Keith Smiley says, "standing still." They are buffeted by a multitude of diseases and insects, droughts, erosion, competition with other trees, the vagaries of weather, and humans. They cannot escape. And still they persevere.

Nora Scarlett has captured for us images of trees that convey the depth of their history of adversity and resilience, and a determination to live that is not only inspiring and thought-provoking, but evokes in me a renewed respect for the complexity of life itself. I think Nora's remarkable images will inspire you, too. ◆

Dr. Paul C. Huth
Director of Research Emeritus and Associate Curator, Daniel Smiley Research Center
Mohonk Preserve

It all started one chilly fall morning in 2005 while out walking in the woods behind my house near New Paltz in New York's Hudson River Valley. I noticed a tree that appeared to be kissing a boulder. Captivated, I returned, lugging my 4 x 5 view camera, studio tripod, dark cloth, film holders and a sack of accessories. With my interest piqued I wondered what other amazing trees were hiding in plain sight, and so began my search. I queried friends, studied maps, and opened my eyes in a new way to the woods around me. The title *Trunks of the Gunks* came to me as I tossed and turned one sleepless night, and the project clicked into existence.

An avid hiker, rock climber, skier and lover of the outdoors, I now had a new, compelling reason to lace up my shoes and don a pack. I hiked extensively around Mohonk Preserve and Minnewaska State Park Preserve on a quest for the elusive trunk, stump, root, burl, log and seedling. As our property borders Mohonk Preserve, this was often just a matter of walking out the back door. I looked for intriguing formations, improbable locations, humorous characteristics, surprising shapes, and other wondrous growths. Such specimens occur frequently at the intersection of rock and root in this geologically unique area, the Shawangunk Mountains (known locally as "the Gunks"), a ridge extending from New Jersey to the Catskills.

As I found a potential subject, I endeavored to clearly portray the remarkable sight as well as create a stunning image. Drawing from my years of studio photography experience, I considered every detail of light and composition. For some scenes I returned many times to capture them in a different light, time of day or season. Early on I switched from the 4 x 5 view camera to a DSLR, which vastly increased my maneuverability. I also sought to show a variety of species, especially the iconic ones of this region such as pitch pine and mountain laurel, and a range of terrain in different seasons. Interestingly, it was often difficult with pitch pine, and I found it impossible with shagbark hickory or mountain laurel, to find an inspiring scene. Instead, the black birch has come to dominate my collection; it's not picky about where it grows and often does so in unusual ways, curving and winding to survive.

Finding the right angle was often a challenge. On a few occasions I could see that where I needed to be was a point ten feet up in the air and ten feet over. Thus, because of unarguable physical limitations, not every wonderful feature was able to be photographed. Using an extremely wide-angle lens allowed me to be close, yet capture a large field of view. In this way I avoided the thicket of other trees that would have obscured the subject. Even so, I frequently wriggled through brush, balanced on a boulder or perched precariously on a steep, muddy embankment searching for the best composition. I was out in the humid, buggy steam bath of summer and in the chilly fall drizzle. I tromped in snowshoes in the cold sparkle of winter and waded through flooded bogs in spring. Nature was not always kind during these forays. Once, as I struggled through branches to the base of a pitch pine, I was attacked and stung repeatedly by ground wasps, even as I fled the area.

The years 2010 and 2011 were the most fruitful, as I devoted myself intensely to the project. From May 2010 to July 2011, I kept an informal shoot log, recording where I went, what I found and other tidbits of information. Following are select excerpts from this log:

10/25 Hike with Robin up crevice thru Giant's Workshop. Great trunk at entrance! Sun is distracting. Need to return.

10/30 142 images! a big day. Hiked up to revisit the "flying" tree over Undercliff Rd. Climbed boulder beside for different view (difficult!!). Kept on going and came home on the stairmaster + Wawarsing. Midafternoon, met Ken at bridge and took Mule to try ANOTHER view of THE overhanging tree on Laurel Ledge. Don't know if better. Returned via Zaidee's Bower and followed stream from Rhododendron Bridge to house.

10/31 Back to Bonticou. Again THE root tangle. Took Northeast Trail back to Clearwater Rd, descended to swamp, found GREAT vine, then back to car.

11/7 Hike along Trapps Rd to Awosting Falls — stop at slabs above Trapps Rd — great light on tiny pitch pine! spent time along stream, trying for a water background.

11/14 Hike up Lower Awosting Rd to lake and around — discover AMAZING beaver activity just beyond beach. Hard to believe tree is still standing. Must return!

11/16 Return to Awosting Lake to check on beaver activity. Speed walk from Lower lot — forecast calling for rain — drizzling on return. freezing cold. So foggy, couldn't see lake. Tree still standing!

11/20 A mad dash from Upper Lot to the beaver tree at Awosting. Still standing. Shot a few others.

11/28 Back to Awosting to look at beaver activity — Tree is down! There is a new one forming a bit farther. Need to keep watch on it. Hiked out the Lower Awosting Rd, but on return, detoured via Jenny Lane trail, then cut back to Lower Rd.

1/17 Snowshoe from Peter's Kill parking to Lost Pond (or Hidden Pond). First checked out potential interesting burl along cliff base to the right. Found it. Not so great now. Maybe with a backdrop of green. Shot tiny seedlings in snow, "wrinkled" snow, the "whale" above cave on end of Lost Pond that Lowell and friends found, and one neat tree on the return (almost at parking lot).

1/20 Snowshoe early morning after ice storm. Bluebird day. Ice on branches — falling chunks — beautiful — scary. Wandered thru woods. Found a few possible "trunks".

4/27 started off early and returned to Keith's tree for morning light. Came home and set off to capture sprouting acorns — the amazing pink color — this year there are TONS! Attempted to shoot the root meadow again (just down Oakwood).

5/18 Ken reported a tree near Coxing, so we went — cool tree but hard to shoot — Nearby found amazing trunk with metal hoop grown into it.

6/28 Left from upper Minnewaska lot and went to end of lake and down Millbrook Cross trail, looking to put mountain laurel in some photographs. Borderline too late. Hard to find anything. Did work on a tree where trail crosses the Peter's Kill, balancing on slimy rocks to get a good angle, hoping not to fall in — By dumb luck, found great pitch pine "tangle" by main overlook at lake (where 2nd hotel was).

7/7 Hike with Ken. Start at Coxing, up Kings Lane past Lost City and kept going — eventually intersecting old logging rd — go left down to the Peter's Kill. Great swimming hole. Bushwhack up Peter's Kill till junction w/blue High Peter's Kill trail. Amazing terrain — but dappled sunlight + dark flat hemlock forest limited shooting. Rhododendrons blooming. Go back on foggy day.

Back home, and after downloading the files, the long tedious hours of sorting, labeling, evaluating, picking and winnowing began. I made between 5 and 75 exposures for every subject, and for every image in this book there are at least 20 that were weeded out. After editing for the most promising images and selecting the strongest, I then tackled the process of converting the faceless pixels into luscious photographs. Working in the "electronic darkroom," I tweaked lights and darks, color and contrast, and made other subtle adjustments so that the final images would reflect my vision and satisfy my artistic standards. The number of hours I happily hiked in the outdoors pale in comparison to those spent hunched in front of a screen.

I devoted my creative energy to this series of photographs for over ten years and amassed a sizable collection of these "trunks." As the body of work grew and coalesced, there were exhibitions and slide shows, so I needed to organize the collection. Staring at hundreds of these images, I realized they fell into distinct categories, which eventually became the sections of this book. In the "Smile" section, we encounter images that through a unique combination of light, shape, texture and even blemish, register as creatures to our eye. I did not start out seeking them. I do not like cutesy images, and these could easily have become that. But they found me. Sometimes it is only by not looking that one can see.

I always knew it had to be a book. At exhibitions people repeatedly asked, "Why don't you make a book?" "Have you thought about making a book?" This haunted me. I made some feeble and unsuccessful attempts to make it happen, but my background in commercial advertising photography was of little help in navigating the publishing world. I sent out feelers, followed many leads, researched literary agents, publishers, and submission guidelines. I attended seminars, made prototypes, and investigated self-publishing resources, despairing that any-thing would ever come of it. And finally it has.

In those hundreds of hours hiking the Gunks, I became awed at how life perseveres despite formidable handicaps, how it adapts to adversity and how it succeeds in astonishing ways. Tiny seedlings emerge from small cracks in rock, sprouting a handful of needles or tender leaves, knowing only to keep trying to grow. Enormous hemlocks hang off ledges, improbably rooted to something, looking as if they shouldn't be upright, and yet … there they are. Roots protrude out of the ground in a preposterous manner, and I stand there in amazement and wonder how they got that way.

I offer these images in the hope that the reader will enjoy viewing them as much as I delighted in creating them. ◆

ROCKS AND ROOTS

The lovely white rock encountered in this region forming ledges, slabs, crevices, outcroppings, cliffs and talus fields is Shawangunk conglomerate, a uniquely hard and durable sedimentary rock. This rock was formed from quartz pebbles and grains of sand that were deposited in a shallow sea covering the area during the Silurian Period, 420 million years ago, as the ancient Taconic Mountains were worn down by erosion. The weight of overlying sediments cemented these deposits into a hard, erosion-resistant layer about 500 feet thick. It overlays the older Martinsburg Formation, a 10,000-foot layer of soft shale created from sediment deposited 465 million years ago in an earlier ancient sea during the Ordovician Period.

Many more layers of limestone and sandstone formed above the conglomerate during the ensuing periods but have since eroded away. Tectonic activity, causing folding and uplifting, combined with erosion over that mind-boggling expanse of time to dramatically shape and transform the terrain. Most recently, glaciation, with ice up to a mile thick (the last glacier receded a mere 14,000 years ago), scoured and polished the bedrock, creating the landscape we see today. Many of the ledges, detached blocks, and rock walls seen in this book are the result of the freeze/thaw cycle that causes the vertical joint cracks to expand, loosen, separate and ultimately collapse the precipices into talus. Today, rock climbers flock to the sheer cliffs to enjoy the quality rock that forms interesting overhangs, pinnacles, corners and faces, posing challenges to beginners and experts alike.

The Gunks contain a surprising abundance of natural features and diversity of vegetation. There are streams, wetlands, swamps, waterfalls, ice caves and the five sky lakes (Mohonk Lake, Lake Minnewaska, Lake Awosting, Mud Pond and Lake Maratanza), formed when the glaciers last receded. About twenty miles long and six miles wide, this relatively small area supports many vegetation zones, from the ridge-top pine barren community, a unique and rare forest type with little soil to support vegetation, to somewhat lower slopes that host mountain laurel, blueberry bushes and larger pitch pines. Descending a bit farther one starts to see white pine, black birch, chestnut oak, sassafras and striped maple. With the deeper soils found on lower slopes, larger trees such as maple, oak, birch, beech, hickory and especially hemlock, are some of the many species that find a home. Lichens, organisms comprised of a fungus in symbiosis with an alga, are found growing on bare rock, requiring no soil at all.

The tree species shown in these photographs are mostly black birch, hemlock and pitch pine. The latter is the iconic tree of the region — the twisted, scraggly, stunted, picturesque profile seen along the white ridge-top slabs eking out an existence in a harsh environment. Also depicted are red oak, red maple, white birch, yellow birch and ash. A few images reveal massive examples of American grape. Although not a tree, its vine nevertheless can become tree-like in size.

This region, with its dramatic cliffs, panoramic ridge-top plateaus and jumbled talus slopes, has been called one of "Earth's Last Great Places" by the Nature Conservancy. For a photographer, inspiration abounds at every precipitous overhang, craggy boulder face, shimmering lake vista, and magical fern glen. ◆

The Shawangunk Mountains or "The Gunks," is a ridge of bedrock in Ulster, Sullivan, and Orange counties in New York State, extending approximately from the northernmost point of New Jersey to the Catskill Mountains.

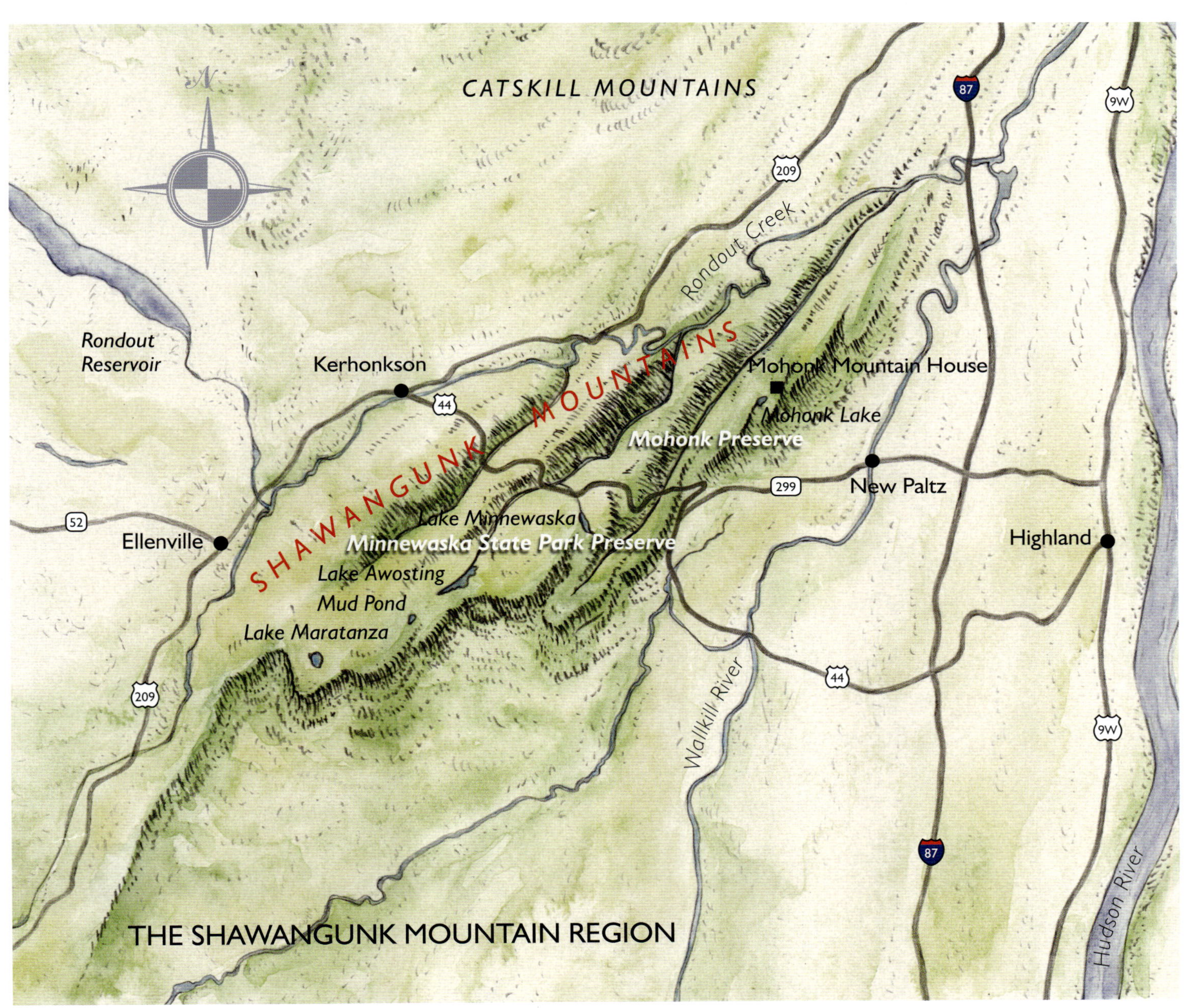

CATSKILL MOUNTAINS
Rondout Creek
Rondout Reservoir
Kerhonkson
SHAWANGUNK MOUNTAINS
Mohonk Mountain House
Mohonk Lake
Mohonk Preserve
New Paltz
Ellenville
Lake Minnewaska
Minnewaska State Park Preserve
Lake Awosting
Mud Pond
Lake Maratanza
Highland
Wallkill River
Hudson River
THE SHAWANGUNK MOUNTAIN REGION

EMBARK

MOVE

TURN

ROOT

DINE

NO
TRESPASSING

POSTED
NO HUNTING
OR
TRESPASSING

HANG

SMILE

BEGIN

END

ABOUT THE AUTHOR

Nora Scarlett discovered her passion for photography in high school when on a whim she enrolled in an introductory course. While attending UC Berkeley during the exciting and turbulent early seventies, she worked as a photojournalist for the campus press and became hooked.

Nora moved to New York City in 1976 and began assisting several respected photographers, learning both technical and studio management skills. Inspired by large-format cameras and studio lighting, she discovered a talent for creating still-life photographs. After many hours in the studio developing her craft and style, themes emerged that still define her work: bold use of color and light; elegant and sometimes quirky composition; a fascination with making ordinary objects beautiful; and developing concepts that result in a series of images. Early on she created an alphabet, "The Scarlett Letters," an ambitious project spanning many years and resulting in twenty-six images depicting each letter in a simple, still-life composition.

By the mid-1980s Nora was shooting major advertising assignments, working with leading agencies and talented art directors on well-known campaigns for clients such as American Express, The Gap, Reebok, Kodak, IBM, AT&T, Nickelodeon, General Foods, Swissair and Knoll. She won numerous awards from the Art Director's Club, the One Show, the Clios, and Print Magazine. That era was intense and hectic, yet exciting and inspiring for her.

After twenty years and the birth of two children, Nora was ready for a calmer pace. She and her family moved to the New Paltz area in 1998, buying a home in the woods bordering Mohonk Preserve — still a convenient commute to New York City. With both children grown now, she has more time to focus on personal projects and to pursue photography in a less commercial way.

Nora continues to love making photographs, working in her thoughtful and deliberate manner whether in the studio or in the woods. ◆

MP: Mohonk Preserve   **MMH:** Mohonk Mountain House   **MSPP:** Minnewaska State Park Preserve

Front Cover: *Oak with Boulder*, 10/27/05, private land

Title Page: *Labyrinth Root*, 11/29/11, along the Labyrinth Path, MMH **

Dedication: *Golden Sapling on Rock*, 10/07/16, Forest Drive, MMH

Page 14: *Hemlock Corner*, 5/10/10, Laurel Ledge Road, MP **

Page 15: *Overhanging Hemlocks*, 10/30/10, on Laurel Ledge Road, MP (right tree fell down in 2015)

Page 16: *Northern Trunk*, 11/06/10, Waterworks area, MP

Page 17: *Giant's Rock and Root*, 10/26/10, at lower entrance to Giant's Workshop, MP **

Page 18: *Cedar Drive Fungus*, 8/23/10, on Cedar Drive, MP

Page 19: *Minnewaska Yellow Birch*, 9/17/10, on Hamilton Point Carriageway, MSPP **

Page 20: *Pitch Pines over Mohonk Lake*, 10/17/10, near Pine Bluff, MMH

Page 21: *Trapps Pitch Pine Panorama*, 10/14/10, along the top of the Trapps, MP

Page 22: *Birch over Boulder*, 11/29/11, along Spring Path, MMH **

Page 23: *Glory Hill Maple*, 10/17/10, in field above Glory Hill Road, MP **

Page 24: *Undercliff Winter*, 1/19/11, on Undercliff Road, MP **

Page 25: *Pitch Pine with Lake*, 11/14/10, along the south side of Lake Awosting, MSPP

Page 26–27: *Minnewaska Pitch Pine on Rock*, 6/28/11, above Lake Minnewaska near site of old hotel, MSPP

Page 28: *Roots on Mossy Boulder*, 10/03/12, above Lake Minnewaska Carriageway, MSPP

Page 29: *Trunk in Talus*, 7/09/10, above Undercliff Road, MP

Page 30: *Peter's Kill Primeval*, 10/09/10, just off High Peter's Kill Trail, MSPP

Page 31: *Peter's Kill Ledge*, 10/09/10, just off High Peter's Kill Trail, MSPP

Page 32: *Pitch Pine and White Slabs*, 10/31/10, Northeast Trail, MP **

Page 33: *Birch on Wooded Slope*, 5/29/11, near Eagle Cliff Carriage Road, MMH

Page 34: *Weathered Birch*, 4/22/11, near Sunset Path, MMH

Page 35: *Split Trunk in Leaves*, 11/18/13, below Upper Awosting Carriageway, MSPP

Page 36: *Cathedral Hemlock Arch*, 5/29/11, Cathedral Path, MP **

Page 37: *Rock Rift Twirl*, 11/03/10, on Rock Rift Trail, MMH (broken off since photo taken)

Page 38: *Halloween Vine*, 10/31/10, near Clearwater Road, MP

Page 39: *Mine Hole Vine*, 10/17/12, along Upper Mine Hole Trail, MSPP **

Page 40: *Autumn Angled Ash*, 10/28/10, Awosting Reserve, MSPP

Page 41: *Split Rock Trunk*, 11/13/10, Split Rock at Coxing, MP **

Page 42: *Late Fall Double Maple*, 11/08/11, just below Hamilton Point Carriageway, MSPP

Page 43: *Hemlock in Swamp*, 12/02/11, Rhododendron Swamp, MP

Page 44: *New Year's Pinnacle and Trees*, 1/01/12, in the talus above Forest Drive, MMH

Page 45: *Winter Trunk and Sky*, 1/17/11, near the Red Loop Trail, MSPP

Page 46: *Birch and Ferns*, 7/07/11, near Kings Lane, MP

Page 47: *Folded Trunk*, 5/14/13, Awosting Reserve, MSPP

Page 48: *Overcliff Root Detail*, 6/26/11, Overcliff Road, MP **

Page 49: *Bonticou Black Birch*, 8/23/10, Bonticou Ascent Path, MP **

Page 50: *Root Meadow*, 4/27/11, Oakwood Drive, MP

Page 51: *Sleepy Hollow Yellow Birch*, 10/14/10, Sleepy Hollow, MP

Page 52: *Roots with Lichen*, 7/07/11, along the Peter's Kill

Page 53: *Root Connection*, 7/07/11, along the Peter's Kill

Page 54: *Clearwater Birch*, 5/01/11, near Clearwater Road, MP

Page 55: *New Year Roots*, 1/01/12, just off Duck Pond Trail, MP

Page 56: *Castle Point Red Maple*, 7/07/10, on Castle Point Carriageway, MSPP (as of 2016 tree has almost completely engulfed the trail marker)

Page 57: *Peter's Kill Plank and Branch*, 7/08/10, on the High Peter's Kill trail, MSPP (bridge was repaired soon after)

Page 58: left to right: *No Trespassing*, 9/30/11, MP; *Posted No Hunting*, 10/10/10, Loop Road in Sam's Point area, MSPP; *Maple with Blue Marker*, 5/31/13, Castle Point Carriageway, MSPP

Page 59: top to bottom: *Yellow Trailmarker on Oak*, 7/07/10, Hamilton Point Carriageway, MSPP (as of 2016 the marker is almost completely engulfed); *Red Trailmarker and Stream*, 4/23/13, Awosting Falls Carriageway, MSPP

** easily viewed from indicated location

The location information is correct to the
best of my knowledge based on notes, recent
observation, camera metadata and memory.
However, the outdoors is forever in flux. With
the passing of time, the terrain changes as trees
fall down, logs rot, saplings grow and trails get
rerouted and renamed.

ACKNOWLEDGMENTS

I wish to thank my friends and family who contributed their ideas, support and help in so many ways with this project: Keith LaBudde, Annie O'Neill, Pril Smiley, Paul Huth, Mary Ann Loschi, Ken Deutschlander, Lowell Deutschlander and Robin Scarlett.

I am especially indebted to my daughter, Zoe Borris, who sat patiently for hours helping weed through batches of new images and winnow out the winners. I welcomed her excellent judgment and perceptive eye. As a hiking partner, Zoe noticed several of these trunks that had escaped my gaze. She also has been an invaluable resource when revising bios, press releases and artist's statements, and she took the photograph of me that appears in this book. ◆

OF THE ELEMENTS

VIII			IB	IIB	IIIA	IVA	VA	VIA	VIIA	VIIIA
										4.003 **He** 2
					10.81 **B** 5	12.011 **C** 6	14.007 **N** 7	15.999 **O** 8	18.998 **F** 9	20.179 **Ne** 10
					26.982 **Al** 13	28.086 **Si** 14	30.9738 **P** 15	32.06 **S** 16	35.453 **Cl** 17	39.948 **Ar** 18
58.933 **Co** 27	58.71 **Ni** 28		63.546 **Cu** 29	65.37 **Zn** 30	69.72 **Ga** 31	72.59 **Ge** 32	74.922 **As** 33	78.96 **Se** 34	79.904 **Br** 35	83.80 **Kr** 36
102.906 **Rh** 45	106.4 **Pd** 46		107.868 **Ag** 47	112.40 **Cd** 48	114.82 **In** 49	118.69 **Sn** 50	121.75 **Sb** 51	127.60 **Te** 52	126.904 **I** 53	131.30 **Xe** 54
192.22 **Ir** 77	195.09 **Pt** 78		196.967 **Au** 79	200.59 **Hg** 80	204.37 **Tl** 81	207.2 **Pb** 82	208.981 **Bi** 83	(209) **Po** 84	(210) **At** 85	(222) **Rn** 86

151.96 **Eu** 63	157.25 **Gd** 64	158.925 **Tb** 65	162.50 **Dy** 66	164.930 **Ho** 67	167.26 **Er** 68	168.934 **Tm** 69	173.04 **Yb** 70	174.97 **Lu** 71
(243) **Am** 95	(247) **Cm** 96	(247) **Bk** 97	(251) **Cf** 98	(254) **Es** 99	(253) **Fm** 100	(256) **Md** 101	(253) **No** 102	(257) **Lr** 103